S0-ENV-004

JUL 29 2010

DISCARDED

SOCCER'S GREATEST STARS

Michael Hurley

**Heinemann Library
Chicago, Illinois**

www.heinemannraintree.com
Visit our website to find out more information about Heinemann-Raintree books.

To order:
☎ Phone 888-454-2279
🖷 Visit www.heinemannraintree.com to browse our catalog and order online.

© 2010 Heinemann Library
an imprint of Capstone Global Library, LLC
Chicago, Illinois

All rights reserved. No part of this publication may be reproduced or transmitted in any form or by any means, electronic or mechanical, including photocopying, recording, taping, or any information storage and retrieval system, without permission in writing from the publisher.

Edited by Kate de Villiers, Catherine Clarke, and Megan Cotugno
Designed by Steve Mead and Debbie Oatley
Picture research by Hannah Taylor
Originated by Dot Gradations Ltd
Printed and bound in China by CTPS

14 13 12 11 10
10 9 8 7 6 5 4 3 2 1

Library of Congress Cataloging-in-Publication Data
Hurley, Michael, 1979-
  Soccer's greatest stars / Michael Hurley.
    p. cm. -- (The World Cup)
  Includes bibliographical references and index.
  ISBN 978-1-4329-3451-4 (hc)
  1. Soccer players--Biography. 2. World Cup (Soccer) I. Title.
  GV942.7.A1H87 2009
  796.3340922--dc22
  [B]
                              2009005269

Acknowledgments
The author and publishers are grateful to the following for permission to reproduce copyright material: © KPT Power Photos **background image**; Action Images pp. **10** (Richard Heathcote Livepic), **13**, **14** (MSI), **15**, **18** (Sporting Pictures/Tony Marshall), **27** (Tony O'Brien); Corbis pp. **22 & 23** (TempSport/© Christian Liewig); Getty Images pp. **4 & 5** (Popperfoto), **7** (Popperfoto/Rolls Press), **9 & 21** (AFP), **16** (Hulton Archive), **19** (AFP/Damien Meyer), **20** (Bob Thomas), **24** (Bob Thomas); PA Photos pp. **11** (S&G and Barratts), **17 & 26** (© Empics/Peter Robinson); Reuters pp. **6** (Roberto Jayme), **12** (Chor Sokunthea), **25** (Action Images/Jordan Murph); Shutterstock pp. **28 & 29** (© Gordan), **background image** (© Nikola I).

Cover photograph of England vs. Japan, International Friendly Match, City of Manchester Stadium, June 1, 2004, reproduced with permission of Rex Features/Jed Leicester.

Every effort has been made to contact copyright holders of material reproduced in this book. Any omissions will be rectified in subsequent printings if notice is given to the publisher.

All the Internet addresses (URLs) given in this book were valid at the time of going to press. However, due to the dynamic nature of the Internet, some addresses may have changed, or sites may have changed or ceased to exist since publication. While the author and publisher regret any inconvenience this may cause readers, no responsibility for any such changes can be accepted by either the author or the publisher.

CONTENTS

The World Cup 4
Pelé 6
Garrincha 8
Eusebio 10
Bobby Charlton 12
Franz Beckenbauer 14
Johan Cruyff 16
Michel Platini 18
Diego Maradona 20
Zinedine Zidane 22
David Beckham 24
Other Great Players 26
World Cup All-Star 11 28
Find Out More 30
Glossary 31
Index 32

Some words are shown in the text in bold, **like this**. You can find out what they mean by looking in the glossary on page 31.

THE WORLD CUP

The **FIFA** World Cup is the most important soccer **tournament** in the world. There have been 18 World Cup tournaments. In 1930 the first World Cup was held in Uruguay, in South America. Uruguay hosted the tournament because its team was the current Olympic soccer champion. National teams from around the world were invited to take part. Only 13 teams participated, including France, Brazil, Argentina, and the United States. Uruguay beat Argentina in the final.

The 2010 World Cup will be held in South Africa and will feature 32 teams. It is the first time that the competition has been held in Africa.

Soccer's greatest stars

The 1958 World Cup was the sixth World Cup tournament. It was held in Sweden, in Europe. An amazing team from Brazil won this tournament. Brazil had a 17-year-old **forward** named Pelé. Pelé had a great tournament. He scored six goals—two of them in the final. Pelé went on to play for Brazil in three more World Cups. He was probably the first real soccer star. He was famous throughout the world. . . and still is today!

France's Just Fontaine also had a very successful tournament in 1958. He finished as top goal scorer, with 13 goals. His record for goals scored in a World Cup still stands today. The World Cup has seen many great players since that 1958 tournament.

A crowd of 80,000 at the Montevideo Estadio Centenario watches the first World Cup final, held in 1930.

PELÉ (BRAZIL)

STATS

DATE OF BIRTH: 10/23/1940
POSITION: FORWARD
WORLD CUP APPEARANCES: 14
WORLD CUP GOALS: 12

Edson Arantes do Nascimento is better known to soccer fans around the world as Pelé. Pelé played in four **FIFA** World Cups and was part of a World Cup–winning Brazil team three times. Pelé had amazing soccer skills. He was quick and strong and had a very powerful **shot**. Pelé was a complete player. This means that he could run, shoot, pass, steal, and head the ball very well. He could do things with a soccer ball that other players could only dream of.

Although Pelé retired from soccer in 1977, he is still one of the most famous soccer players in the world. This photograph was taken in 2008, at the opening of an exhibition about his life.

Pelé was only 17 years old when he played in his first World Cup, in 1958. Even then, he was Brazil's star player. Pelé's goals helped Brazil win its first World Cup. The World Cup in 1966, however, was not very successful for Brazil and Pelé. Brazil went out of the **tournament** at the first stage, after Pelé was injured.

Playing without Pelé

Brazil had many good players. Fans from all over the world admired the entertaining soccer they played. In 1962 Brazil won its second World Cup in Chile, South America. Pelé only played in the first game. He was injured and had to watch from the sidelines as his teammates won the tournament.

World Cup 1970

After disappointment in 1966, the Brazil team was determined to regain the title of world champions. Pelé was in his late twenties. He had matured into a truly great soccer player. He was captain of his country's team and its most important player.

The Brazil team at the 1970 World Cup has been described by soccer fans as the greatest soccer team ever, and Pelé as the greatest player ever. Pelé played in every match for Brazil at the 1970 World Cup. He scored four goals. One of these goals was in the final **versus** Italy. Brazil won the match 4–1, to become world champion again.

The 1970 World Cup was a success for Brazil and Pelé.

GARRINCHA
(BRAZIL)

Garrincha played for Brazil at three **FIFA** World Cups. He was part of the Brazil team that won the trophy in both 1958 and 1962. Although Garrincha was part of the 1958 Brazil World Cup squad, he did not play in the team's first two matches. He was brought into the Brazil team for its last **group match** and played well enough to stay on the team for the rest of the **tournament**. He went on to play in three more matches, including the final.

Garrincha helped Brazil win its first World Cup. Brazil had the two greatest players of the time: Garrincha and Pelé. Garrincha was a different type of player from Pelé: he was a **winger**. He had amazing **dribbling** skills. He was quick and could run past **defenders** with the ball at his feet. It often looked as though the ball was glued to his cleats. His dribbling ability was possibly the best ever.

Goals galore

In the 1962 World Cup, Garrincha was Brazil's best player. When Pelé was injured in Brazil's first match, many supporters thought that Brazil could not win the tournament. Garrincha had other ideas. He was incredible, scoring goals and creating opportunities for other players. At the 1962 World Cup he scored four goals in six matches, and he was officially named the best player of the tournament. He was also the joint top goal scorer. He had proved that Brazil could win without Pelé.

STATS

DATE OF BIRTH: 10/28/1933
POSITION: WINGER
WORLD CUP APPEARANCES: 11
WORLD CUP GOALS: 5

Garrincha (left) dribbles the ball easily past a Welsh defender in the 1958 World Cup quarterfinal.

Little Bird

Garrincha's real name was Manoel Francisco dos Santos. Because he was small, his sister gave him the nickname Garrincha, which means "Little Bird." In addition to being small, Garrincha was also unusual because his legs were different lengths. When he was a teenager many experts thought he would never be able to play professional soccer. This didn't stop Little Bird!

EUSEBIO (PORTUGAL)

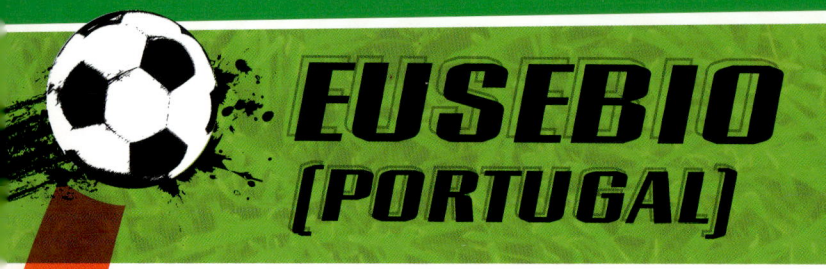

Eusebio is the greatest player in the history of Portuguese soccer. Born in Mozambique, Africa, Eusebio moved to Portugal when he was 18 years old. He made his **debut** for Portugal a year later, and he went on to play for the team 64 times. Eusebio only played in one **FIFA** World Cup, in England in 1966. Eusebio was one of the stars of the **tournament** and was the top goal scorer, with nine goals.

STATS

DATE OF BIRTH: 01/25/1942
POSITION: FORWARD
WORLD CUP APPEARANCES: 6
WORLD CUP GOALS: 9

Eusebio's **club** was Benfica. This statue of him stands outside Benfica's stadium in Lisbon, Portugal, as a reminder of the team's greatest player of all time.

Golden Player

The Portuguese Football [Soccer] Federation named Eusebio its "Golden Player" in 2004 to celebrate 50 years of **UEFA**.

Important goals

Eusebio was a **forward** with lots of **pace** and strength. He also had a very powerful **shot**. His performances in the 1966 World Cup were very good. He helped his team by scoring some important goals. Portugal won its first match 3–1, and then in the second match Eusebio scored one of the goals as the team beat Bulgaria 3–0. Eusebio's goal-scoring carried into the final **group match versus** Brazil. He scored twice, as Portugal knocked the World Cup holders out of the tournament.

Portugal's quarterfinal match was against North Korea. Portugal was expected to beat the Koreans. After 25 minutes Eusebio and his teammates found themselves down 3–0. Eusebio then scored four goals to help his team win the match 5–3. It was an incredible individual performance by the young forward.

*This is just one of the goals that Eusebio scored against North Korea to **inspire** his team to come back and win the match.*

In the semifinal against England, Portugal lost 2–1. Eusebio played well and scored a **penalty** in the last 10 minutes, but it wasn't enough to see his team through to the final. He also scored in the playoff match against the Soviet Union—the other losing semifinalist. Portugal clinched third place in the World Cup, with a 2–1 victory. Eusebio had scored nine goals in six matches. He had also captured the imagination of soccer fans around the world.

BOBBY CHARLTON (ENGLAND)

England's Bobby Charlton was an outstanding **midfielder** and had a very successful soccer career. He played more than 100 times for his country and was part of the England team that won the **FIFA** World Cup in 1966. He is also England's all-time top goal scorer, with 49 goals. Charlton played for England in three World Cups and scored four goals. His performances in 1966 were crucial to England's success.

Bobby Charlton is involved in charity work, such as raising awareness for a landmine charity here in Cambodia.

STATS

DATE OF BIRTH: 10/11/1937
POSITION: MIDFIELDER
WORLD CUP APPEARANCES: 12
WORLD CUP GOALS: 4

Sir Bobby

In addition to being a great player for England, Bobby Charlton was also a great club player. He played for Manchester United, a team in England, for 17 years. He won the **UEFA** European Cup and the English league championship three times. In 1994 Charlton was given a **knighthood** by the queen of England for his services to soccer and charity. His official title is Sir Bobby Charlton.

Along with his 1966 teammates, Bobby Charlton (top right) will always be remembered for England's World Cup victory.

England's greatest moment

Bobby Charlton was a very **consistent** player for his **club** and country. He was always willing to attack the **opposition** and shoot from a distance. Charlton's powerful **shots** were very popular with fans. He scored twice against Portugal in the World Cup semifinal in 1966, and England won that match 2–1. He then helped England to beat West Germany in the final. He didn't score, but he worked very hard for his team, trying to stop the German attacks. His reward was a World Cup winners' medal, and he will always be associated with the greatest result in the history of English soccer.

After finishing his playing career, Bobby Charlton has continued to be involved in soccer. He created soccer schools to help children improve their skills and he has worked as an **ambassador** for English soccer. Like Pelé, he is recognized throughout the world by soccer fans.

FRANZ BECKENBAUER (WEST GERMANY)

Franz Beckenbauer made his **debut** for West Germany in 1965, when he was only 20 years old. He went on to win more than 100 **caps** for his country. Beckenbauer played in three **FIFA** World Cups for West Germany, in 1966, 1970, and 1974, and made 18 appearances. He was a strong, powerful **defender** with good ball control and passing ability.

STATS

DATE OF BIRTH: 09/11/1945
POSITION: DEFENDER
WORLD CUP APPEARANCES: 18
WORLD CUP GOALS: 5

Franz Beckenbauer (in white) challenges for the ball against Holland in the 1974 World Cup.

Beckenbauer's first World Cup appearance was against Switzerland in 1966. He scored two goals in a convincing 5–0 win. As a defender Beckenbauer was not expected to score as many goals as he did. He had a good **tournament** in 1966, when he scored goals in the quarterfinal and semifinal, before West Germany was beaten by England in the final.

At the 1970 World Cup, Beckenbauer and West Germany made it to the semifinals, but were beaten by Italy. In 1974 the World Cup was held in West Germany, and Beckenbauer's team was one of the favorites. West Germany was the **host**, and there was a lot of pressure on Beckenbauer and his teammates. The German fans expected them to win the tournament. With Beckenbauer controlling the play, West Germany coped very well with this added pressure. The team made it to the final, where it beat Holland 2–1 in a close match.

Player and manager

Franz Beckenbauer is one of only two men to have won the World Cup as a player and also as a manager. He was captain of the West German team that won the tournament in 1974 on home soil. He was the manager of West Germany in 1990, when it beat Argentina in the final.

Beckenbauer (second from top left) poses with his team as it celebrates winning the World Cup in 1990.

Der Kaiser

Franz Beckenbauer was given the nickname "Der Kaiser" in the late 1960s. It is German for "The Emperor." This name was meant to describe his **influence** and control on the soccer field.

JOHAN CRUYFF
(HOLLAND)

Johan Cruyff is Holland's most famous, talented, and **influential** player of all time. He had wonderful balance and great ball control. He was able to pass precisely, shoot accurately, and **dribble** the ball confidently. Cruyff made his **club debut** for Ajax, in Holland, when he was only 17 years old, and made his debut for his national team soon after.

STATS

DATE OF BIRTH: 04/25/1947
POSITION: FORWARD
WORLD CUP APPEARANCES: 7
WORLD CUP GOALS: 3

Holland's star player

Cruyff's greatest moment as a player was during the 1974 World Cup in West Germany. Although Holland ended the **tournament** as runner-up, the team played amazing soccer that was popular with fans. In a team full of technically good players, Cruyff was the star. He roamed around the field, causing trouble for the **opposition** and switching positions with his teammates to make the most of his attacking talents.

Even as a very young player, Johan Cruyff (far right) was a star for his club, Ajax.

Cruyff scores the second of his two goals for Holland against Argentina in the 1974 World Cup.

Cruyff scored some memorable goals during the tournament. He scored two of his team's four goals against Argentina in a 4–0 win. He then scored the second goal of the match when Holland beat Brazil 2–0, hitting a stunning **volley** into the net. After the win against Brazil, Holland was in the World Cup final, where it met the **host**, West Germany. Cruyff earned his team a **penalty** in the first few minutes of the final. He was fouled as he dribbled the ball into the penalty area, and Holland took a 1–0 lead from the penalty spot. West Germany then scored two goals to take the lead. Although Holland, with Cruyff trying his hardest, continued to play well, the team could not get back into the match. Holland was beaten 2–1.

Holland's and Ajax's greatest player

Johan Cruyff was Holland's most important player during the 1970s and the most important player for his club, Ajax. Ajax won the **UEFA** European Cup three times in a row, in 1971, 1972, and 1973.

MICHEL PLATINI (FRANCE)

Michel Platini was one the greatest soccer players of all time. He played exceptional soccer to help his team, France, to the **FIFA** World Cup semifinals twice—in 1982 and 1986. Platini was a very skilled **midfielder**. His passing ability was outstanding, and he scored amazing goals from **free kicks**.

STATS

DATE OF BIRTH: 06/21/1955
POSITION: MIDFIELDER
WORLD CUP APPEARANCES: 14
WORLD CUP GOALS: 5

Michel Platini made his World Cup **debut** in 1978, but France could not advance past the **group stage**. Platini and France had a more successful World Cup in 1982. The team was unlucky to lose on **penalties** against West Germany in the semifinal. Platini was one of the best players in the **tournament**. He used his skills and intelligence on the field to create opportunities for his teammates.

Platini plays for his country at the 1986 World Cup.

France's most important player

In 1986 France was one of the favorites for the World Cup, in Mexico. Platini had matured into a world-class midfielder and wanted to help his team win the trophy for the first time. France performed extremely well during the tournament. Platini was the most important player in a very **creative** French midfield. He scored goals in wins against Italy and Brazil, two of the other tournament favorites. France met West Germany again in the semifinal. France lost 2–0 and was out of the World Cup. When Platini retired from playing soccer, at 32 years old, he had won every trophy available in his career except the World Cup.

Staying in soccer

After his career as a player finished, Michel Platini was the manager of the team from France between 1988 and 1992. He worked on the organizing committee of the 1998 World Cup in France. He has also worked as an advisor to Sepp Blatter, the president of FIFA. Platini is now the president of **UEFA**, the Union of European Football [Soccer] Associations.

As UEFA president, Platini presents players from Spain with their medals after they won the Euro 2008 championship.

DIEGO MARADONA (ARGENTINA)

Diego Maradona's soccer career was full of amazing moments and **controversy**. Maradona played for Argentina at four **FIFA** World Cups, playing in 21 matches. He was part of the Argentina team that won the World Cup in Mexico in 1986, and was a losing finalist four years later, in Italy.

STATS
DATE OF BIRTH: 10/30/1960
POSITION: MIDFIELDER
WORLD CUP APPEARANCES: 21
WORLD CUP GOALS: 8

Maradona made his first appearance at a World Cup in 1982, in Spain. He scored his first World Cup goal in a **group match versus** Hungary. Argentina failed to get beyond the second round, and Maradona was ejected (thrown out) in the team's match against Brazil.

Winning the World Cup

The World Cup in 1986 was much more successful for Argentina, and Maradona in particular. Fans watched as the stocky little **midfielder** used his incredible **dribbling** skills and wonderful balance to defeat the **opposition**.

Maradona and his team celebrate winning the World Cup in 1986.

In the quarterfinal against England, Maradona scored both of his team's goals in a 2–1 win. The first was very controversial because he used his hand to score. The goal should have been disqualified. The second goal was one of the greatest ever scored in a World Cup match. Maradona ran half the length of the field and dribbled the ball past six players from the England team before shooting the ball into the goal to score. He had another excellent match against Belgium in the semifinal, scoring twice to take his team into the final.

Argentina beat West Germany 3–2 in the final to win the World Cup. Diego Maradona was named the player of the **tournament** for his amazing performances.

After some thrilling performances in the World Cup in 1986 and 1990, Diego Maradona was sent home in disgrace from the 1994 World Cup, in the United States. He was banned from playing soccer because he failed a drug test. Maradona has always been a controversial figure, but his amazing ability as a soccer player has never been in doubt.

"Goal of the Century"

In a poll on FIFA's website, Diego Maradona's second goal against England in the 1986 World Cup was voted by fans as the "Goal of the Century."

ZINEDINE ZIDANE (FRANCE)

Zinedine Zidane is one of the greatest soccer players of recent times. He played for France at three **FIFA** World Cups. He was the most important and **influential** player for France when it won the World Cup at home in 1998. He was also part of the team from France that lost in the final to Italy in 2006.

STATS

DATE OF BIRTH: 06/23/1972
POSITION: MIDFIELDER
WORLD CUP APPEARANCES: 12
WORLD CUP GOALS: 5

Fans around the world think of Zidane as one of the most talented players to have ever played soccer. He had great balance, **vision**, and passing ability. His performances for France in 1998 were very important to the team's success. France made it through to the semifinals after beating Italy on **penalties**. Because France was playing at home, there was a lot of pressure on the players to succeed.

France made it to the final after a close semifinal match with Croatia that it won 2–1. Zidane did not score, but his calm, confident performance helped his teammates to do well. In the final against Brazil, Zidane was again the most important player for France. He scored two goals in a convincing 3–0 win, and he was named the best player of the World Cup final. The French fans celebrated their team's first ever World Cup win.

Leaving in disgrace

The 2006 final was Zidane's last appearance for France, and the **midfielder's** brilliant career ended in **controversy** when he was ejected from the game. He made headlines around the world for all of the wrong reasons when he head-butted an **opponent** in the chest and was given a **red card**. Despite being ejected in the final, Zidane's great performances meant that he was named player of the **tournament**.

Zidane celebrates after scoring the second goal of the 1998 World Cup final against Brazil.

World Player of the Year

Zinedine Zidane was named the FIFA World Player of the Year three times in his career. The only other player to have achieved this is Brazil's Ronaldo.

DAVID BECKHAM
(ENGLAND)

David Beckham is probably the most famous and popular soccer player in the world. He has played more than 100 times for England and has played in three **FIFA** World Cups. Beckham is famous for his ability to **cross** and shoot the ball accurately. He is also famous for his lifestyle away from soccer.

STATS
DATE OF BIRTH: 05/02/1975
POSITION: MIDFIELDER
WORLD CUP APPEARANCES: 13
WORLD CUP GOALS: 3

Beckham made his first World Cup appearance in France in 1998. He announced his ability to fans around the world by scoring an amazing goal from a **free kick** against Colombia in England's final **group match**. In the next match, against Argentina, he helped to set up a goal for England with a precise pass. The score was 2–2 at halftime. Very early in the second half, Beckham was fouled, and he reacted badly. He was ejected for kicking an **opponent**. England failed to beat Argentina with only 10 players on the field. The team lost on **penalties**, and Beckham was devastated.

Beckham helped England get past the group stage at the 1998 World Cup by scoring this free kick against Colombia. It was his first goal for England.

World Cup revenge

David Beckham was blamed for England's failure to beat Argentina. His response was to prove that he was a great player and important for England. His performances improved, and he became an important player for England for the next 10 years. He was made the England captain in 2001.

Beckham was England's captain during the 2002 and 2006 World Cup **tournaments**. He scored an important penalty against Argentina at the **group stage** in 2002, and England won the match 1–0. He was able to get some revenge after his error in 1998. Unfortunately for Beckham, he never had the chance to lift the World Cup trophy as England's captain. England failed to get past the quarterfinals in 2002 and 2006.

Beckham's soccer schools

David Beckham has set up two soccer schools: one in London, England, and another in Los Angeles, California. These schools aim to develop the skills of young players—the soccer stars of the future!

In addition to his soccer schools, Beckham takes part in charity and community events, such as this one in Hawaii, to encourage youth soccer.

OTHER GREAT PLAYERS

Many great soccer players have played at the **FIFA** World Cup. Unfortunately, some other great players haven't had the chance to shine at the World Cup. Here are just three of them:

George Best (Northern Ireland)

George Best played soccer between 1963 and 1984 and was one of the greatest players in the world. He had amazing **dribbling** skills and could score incredible goals. He could score with either foot or with his head. Northern Ireland did not qualify for the World Cup when he was an international player. It is a shame that more fans did not get to see this talented player in action at a World Cup.

Despite being one of the most talented soccer players of all time, George Best was never able to shine with his Northern Ireland team at a World Cup.

Eric Cantona (France)

Eric Cantona was a skilled, powerful, and confident **forward**. He scored many great goals in his soccer career. He played for France between 1987 and 1994. Cantona did not have the chance to play in a World Cup because France did not qualify for the **tournament** in 1990 and 1994.

Ryan Giggs (Wales)

Ryan Giggs is the most successful soccer player to play in the English **Premier League**. He has won the league title with his team, Manchester United, 11 times. He has also won the European Cup twice. He has been an important player for his **club** and his country for a long time. Giggs tried to help Wales's national team qualify for the World Cup many times, but even with his skills and experience the team did not succeed.

Ryan Giggs and Eric Cantona enjoyed a lot of success with their club, Manchester United.

Common ground

In addition to not having the chance to appear at the World Cup, George Best, Eric Cantona, and Ryan Giggs have something else in common. They have all played for Manchester United, in England. Manchester United is one of the most famous and successful professional soccer clubs in the world.

WORLD CUP ALL-STAR 11

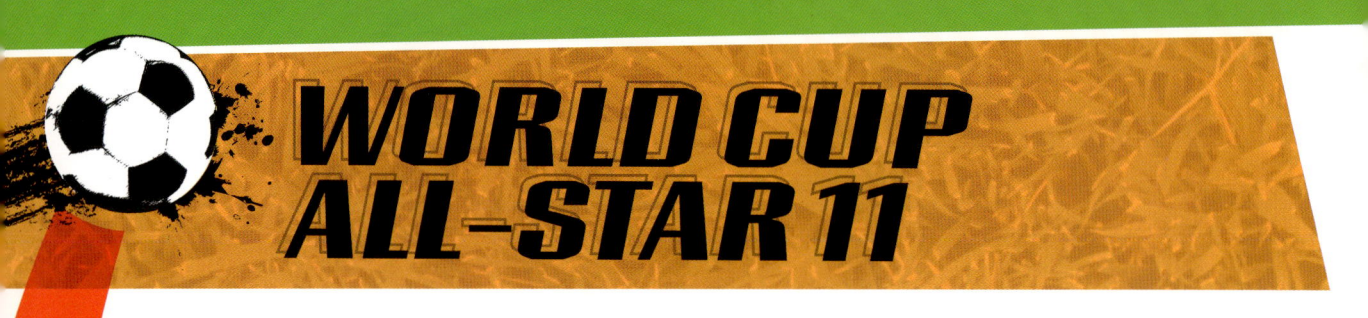

There are too many players who have been outstanding at the World Cup to mention them all in this book. Each country that has been represented at the World Cup has had great players who amazed fans around the world. This diagram is an example of a "dream team," or World Cup **All-Star 11**. See page 30 for resources on some of these amazing players from throughout soccer's history.

1 Dino Zoff
(Italy)
Date of birth: 02/28/1942
Position: Goalkeeper
World Cup appearances: 17
World Cup goals: 0

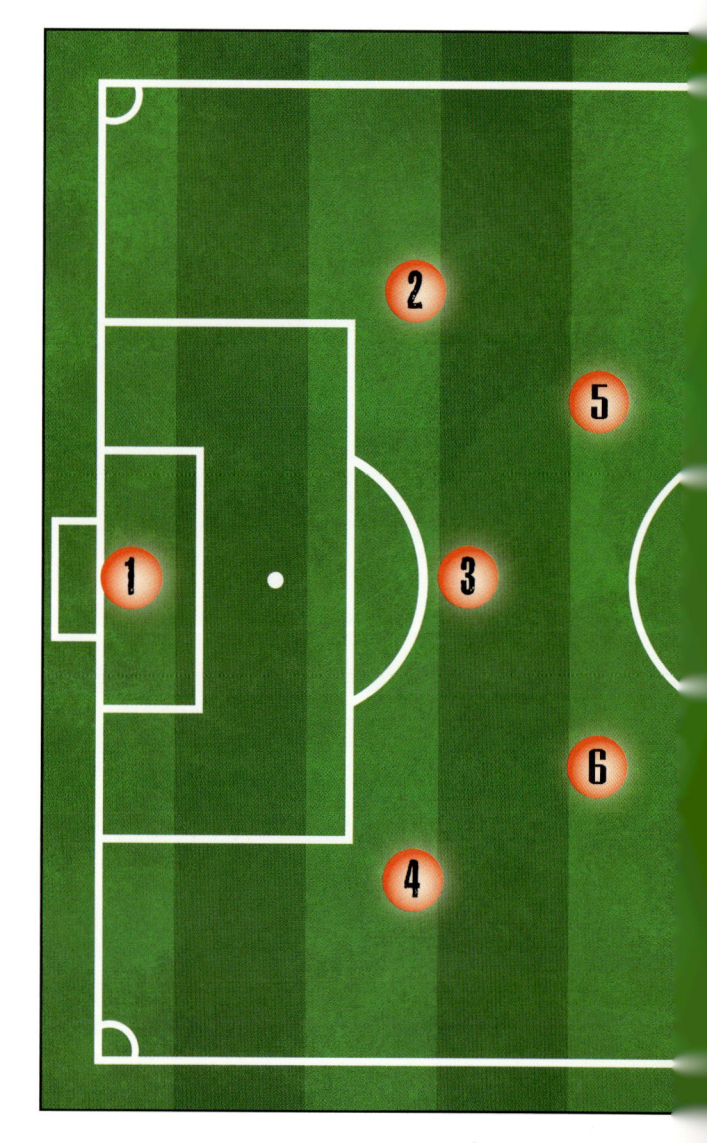

2 Bobby Moore
(England)
Date of birth: 04/12/1941
Position: **Defender**
World Cup appearances: 12
World Cup Goals: 0

3 Franz Beckenbauer
(Germany)
Date of birth: 09/11/1945
Position: Defender
World Cup appearances: 18
World Cup goals: 5

4 Franco Baresi
(Italy)
Date of birth: 05/08/1960
Position: Defender
World Cup appearances: 10
World Cup goals: 0

5 Zinedine Zidane
(France)

Date of birth: 06/23/1972
Position: **Midfielder**
World Cup appearances: 13
World Cup goals: 3

6 Bobby Charlton
(England)

Date of birth: 10/11/1937
Position: Midfielder
World Cup appearances: 12
World Cup goals: 4

7 Johan Cruyff
(Holland)

Date of birth: 04/25/1947
Position: **Forward**
World Cup appearances: 7
World Cup goals: 3

8 Diego Maradona
(Argentina)

Date of birth: 10/30/1960
Position: Midfielder
World Cup appearances: 21
World Cup goals: 8

9 Ronaldo
(Brazil)

Date of birth: 09/22/1976
Position: Forward
World Cup appearances: 19
World Cup goals: 15

10 Pelé
(Brazil)

Date of birth: 10/23/1940
Position: Forward
World Cup appearances: 13
World Cup goals: 12

11 Gerd Muller
(Germany)

Date of birth: 11/03/1945
Position: Forward
World Cup appearances: 13
World Cup goals: 14

FIND OUT MORE

Books to read

Beckham, David. *Beckham: Both Feet on the Ground*. New York: HarperCollins, 2003.

Buckley, Jr., James. *Pelé*. New York: Dorling Kindersley, 2007.

Collie, Ashley Jude. *World of Soccer: A Complete Guide to the World's Most Popular Sport*. New York: Rosen, 2003.

Gifford, Clive. *Soccer: The Ultimate Guide to the Beautiful Game*. Boston: Kingfisher, 2004.

Godsall, Ben. *The Making of a Champion: An International Soccer Star*. Chicago: Heinemann Library, 2005.

Lineker, Gary. *Soccer*. New York: Dorling Kindersley, 2005.

Savage, Jeff. *Amazing Athletes: David Beckham*. Minneapolis: Lerner, 2000.

Shea, Therese. *Greatest Sports Heroes: Soccer Stars*. New York: Children's Press, 2007.

Websites

www.fifa.com
This website has all of the information about the FIFA World Cup. It is great for finding out about your favorite players and teams.

www.ussoccer.com
This is the official website of the U.S. Soccer Federation. It provides news and coverage of all the U.S. teams and players.

GLOSSARY

All-star 11 team containing some of the greatest players of all time

ambassador person who represents or raises awareness of an activity

cap award given to soccer players after playing in an international match

club word used to describe a professional soccer team. Soccer clubs play in national leagues and are different from national teams.

consistent always the same

controversy argument or difference of opinion

creative something new and different

cross when the ball is kicked from the side of the field to the area in front of the goal

debut first appearance. A soccer player's first match is his or her debut.

defender position of a soccer player on the field. Defenders try to stop the opposition from scoring.

dribble running with the ball

FIFA (*Fédération Internationale de Football* [Soccer] *Association*) international organization responsible for soccer around the world

forward position of a soccer player on the field. Forwards try to score goals.

free kick kick of the ball awarded by the referee after a foul

group match a match in the group stage, when teams play each other to decide who will move on to the next stage

group stage stage in a tournament when teams play in groups to decide who will move on to the next stage

host country where a tournament is being played

influence setting a good example that others want to follow

inspire make people feel that they can do something

knighthood award given out by the queen of England

midfielder player positioned in the middle of the field who helps the attacking and defending players

opposition team that you are playing against

pace speed

penalty the referee gives a penalty if a foul happens in the penalty area, an 18-yard rectangular area surrounding the goal. The ball is placed on a spot 12 yards from the goal, and only the goalkeeper is allowed to stop the shot.

Premier League league of professional soccer clubs in England

red card card shown by the referee to a player, usually for a dangerous foul. The player leaves the field.

shot kick of the ball toward the goal

tournament organized number of matches that lead to a final. The winner of the final game wins the tournament.

UEFA (Union of European Football [Soccer] Associations) organization responsible for European soccer

versus against

vision ability to think about and picture something before it happens

volley kick of the soccer ball before it touches the ground

winger position of a player on the field. Wingers play wide on the field and usually try to create chances for their team to score.

INDEX

Ajax 16
Argentina 4, 15, 17, 20–21, 24, 25, 29

Baresi, Franco 28
Beckenbauer, Franz 14–15, 28
Beckham, David 24–25
Belgium 21
Benfica 10
Best, George 26, 27
Blatter, Sepp 19
Brazil 4, 5, 6, 11, 17, 19, 20, 22, 23, 29
Bulgaria 11

Cantona, Eric 27
charity work 12, 25
Charlton, Bobby 12–13, 29
Colombia 24
controversies 20, 21, 23
Croatia 22
Cruyff, Johan 16–17, 29

defenders 14–15, 28
dribbling skills 8, 16, 21, 26
drug tests 21

England 11, 12–13, 14, 21, 24–25, 28, 29
European Cup 12, 17, 27
Eusebio 10–11

FIFA 19
Fontaine, Just 5
forwards 5, 6–7, 10–11, 16–17, 27, 29
fouls 17, 24

France 4, 5, 18–19, 22–23, 27, 29
free kicks 18, 24

Garrincha 8–9
Giggs, Ryan 27
Goal of the Century 21
goal scoring 5, 8, 10, 11, 12, 17, 18, 26, 28, 29
goalkeepers 28

Holland 15, 16–17, 29
Hungary 20

Italy 7, 15, 19, 22, 28

managers 15, 19
Manchester United 12, 27
Maradona, Diego 20–21, 29
midfielders 12–13, 18–25, 29
Moore, Bobby 28
Muller, Gerd 29

North Korea 11
Northern Ireland 26

Pelé 5, 6–7, 8, 13, 29
penalties 11, 17, 18, 22, 24, 25
Platini, Michel 18–19
Portugal 10–11, 13
Premier League 27

red cards 23
Ronaldo 23, 29

soccer schools 13, 25
South Africa 5

Soviet Union 11
Spain 19
Switzerland 14

UEFA 10, 12, 17, 19
United States 4
Uruguay 4

Wales 9, 27
West Germany 13, 14–15, 17, 18, 19, 21, 28, 29
wingers 8–9
World Cup 1930 4
World Cup 1958 5, 7, 8, 9
World Cup 1962 8
World Cup 1966 7, 10, 11, 12, 13, 14
World Cup 1970 7, 14, 15
World Cup 1974 14, 15, 16–17
World Cup 1978 18
World Cup 1982 18, 20
World Cup 1986 18, 19, 20, 21
World Cup 1990 15, 21, 27
World Cup 1994 21, 27
World Cup 1998 19, 22, 23, 24
World Cup 2002 25
World Cup 2006 22, 25
World Cup 2010 5
World Cup All-Star 11 28–29
World Player of the Year 23

Zidane, Zinedine 22–23, 29
Zoff, Dino 28